Boxes of Bees

Erica Miller

Boxes of Bees

ISBN:1523273674
ISBN-13:9781523273676

DEDICATION

I would like to dedicate this book to my cat, Hazel Grace, my family, including my mom, Kimberly Henry, my brother, Hunter Henry, and my grandparents, Don and Cindy Henry, my wonderful mentor, Eric Tally, the Onslow County Beekeeping Association and everyone around me . . . . except neighbor Steve.

Boxes of Bees

CONTENTS

Boxes of Bees

ACKNOWLEDGMENTS

I would like to thank the Onslow County Beekeeping association, and their amazing president, Eric Tally, for giving me the opportunity to become a beekeeper, my wonderful mother, for driving me back and forth for the meetings, Sunday sessions, and much more, and all my English teachers for teaching me how to properly write.

Boxes of Bees

1
HOW I STARTED

How exactly does someone start to "keep bee's"? Is it in their genes from generations past? How does someone become a beekeeper, and how in the world do you find yourself here? I never expected to become a beekeeper. I did not really think about beekeeping, my mom talked about bee's, I knew beekeepers were very important, but knowing that bee's were important seemed enough for me; at the time. When my mom came home with the information on the apprenticeship program with the Onslow County Beekeeping Association, I really did not give it a second thought. I thought about it, and thought it was interesting, however I did not see it in my future; boy was I wrong!

The program was created to encourage a younger generation of beekeepers, as the bee's need people in order to live. A lot of the beekeeping generation is getting older, they need some young blood. Since most wild beehives are gone at this point, the bees need someone to take care of them; that's where you and I come in. Since bees in the wild are slowly dwindling away, beekeepers become more important every day. Most bees in today's world are from a beekeeper's hive, if you see a bee in the wild, it's probably more than likely living in a man-made box; rather than an all-natural beehive.

My mom encouraged me to fill out the application, so I did. I sent in my application a day late, my mother and I not realizing that the application was due so soon. We emailed it to the Association so it would get there sooner, rather than using snail mail. My anticipation was high because I didn't believe they would accept my application, due to it being late. I was sure, since my application was late, it would show bad character, and why in the world would they want an apprentice with bad character?

But they did accept it, and I was elated! Sometimes it's okay to be late!

The very next day we got an email saying that my application was accepted, and that they would be going over them and telling us if I made it as soon as possible.

I checked the mail one day, not expecting anything for me, but right there on the envelope was my name, right above my address, from the OCBA.
I made it into the program, along with two other apprentices from Onslow County, all aged 13-19.
First things first, we had to take a class on beekeeping. At the end of the class, we had to take a test, which would make us certified beekeepers within the state of North Carolina.

We all passed, in fact, I made a higher score than my mother! A few weeks after taking the test, we got our certificates in the mail, proudly sporting our names proving that we were certified beekeepers. My mom and I then proudly framed them for all to see.

2
HANDLING BEES

How did I feel being around all those bees? The first time I dealt with bees was kind of unnerving, but not at all frightening. But let's go back a few steps, you have to get the bees before you get the honey. Before getting the bees into the hives, you have to build the hives. Sometime prior to getting my bee's, my mentor and I got together and built our boxes.

All of the apprentices were there, Kyle and I, shared a wonderful mentor named, Mr. Eric Tally, who was also the president of OCBA. Shortly after we arrived that day, we started working on our hives excitedly, hammering nailing and gluing the jigsaw

6

like puzzles together. We had to build them in the correct formation to make what ended up being beautiful boxes, perfectly shaped and sized for the bees that would soon come to reside in them. When I was finished, I had three hive boxes where my bee colony would live, and a nuke to raise queens in.

After our hives were built, they had to be painted. I wanted mine to be very appealing to the eye, so I settled on a teal color. I decorated them with flowers, leaves, trees, and lady bugs. They were very pretty, but the thing that would become the most beautiful about them was the amazing society that would soon be thriving inside of them.

My bees were ordered by the OCBA and they came inside of a box. When we got the bee's, we had to move them from the box they came in to the hive they would call home. When we transferred our bees from the mailing box into the hives, it was relatively simple. You have to transfer the bees by putting the box they came in, into the hive, along with the queen that they came with. There is a little queen cage that has the queen bee and a piece of candy in it. The queen comes with nurse bee's inside the small cage and you hang this cage on the inside of the frames. The colony will eat the candy out of the cage and the queen will come out. I learned that you hang this candy side down when inserting a new queen. My queen looked happy in her cage when we hung her there that day.

The bees would be kept in Mr. Eric's bee yard for the first year of my beekeeping, that way when we worked with them we would have the guidance we needed. Mr. Eric was very helpful throughout the entire process, and I couldn't have asked for a kinder, more patient man to guide me through my experience.

From that point on, all the bees required was simple maintenance. Giving them sugar water, making sure they didn't go "queen less", ensuring that everything was going well, and most of the time, it was.

Very quickly our small one box hives, became three box hives, and they only got bigger after that.
Soon we had enough room to make some nukes, which raises queens. Raising your own queen allows you to more easily build bee colonies without having to go through the hassle of ordering a new queen. You can use the queen in your nuke to replace a queen that has died, and trust me; you will want to find a queen quickly if your hive has lost its queen bee.

3
WHY I DO IT

In the beginning of my experience, I was only doing this because it was what my mom wanted, but I soon learned to enjoy it much more than that. My mother wanted bees for years, but we never got any. She always talked about how it can be "our way to help save the world." She learned about the mentorship program by researching local beekeepers. When she heard about the program, she jumped on her chance to get me involved! After I started taking care of my bees, it was very enjoyable. Every Sunday afternoon we would gather in Mr. Eric's bee yard to check up on the bees and make sure they were all okay, then record what we did to make sure we would have a good record in case something ever went terribly wrong.

I think that Sunday is the perfect day for beekeeping, as Sunday is the day of the Lord, and there is no other time to be close to nature as the day of rest.

The amazing thing about beekeeping is that you are able to be incredibly close to things that most people never even know about. Every time you go in the hive you can see something different. Whether it is as simple as a beautiful queen with a bundle of bees around her, or as wonderful as the birth of a worker bee.

It is not only the remarkable bees that make beekeeping amazing, but the structures they manage to build. These simple creatures build glamourous society's, simply using bits of wood and foundation.

4
BEES ARE LEAVING

Why are bee's disappearing? What most people don't realize is how "bad off" bees really are. There are many diseases, mites, scavengers, and pesticides that harm bees, and can wipe out entire hives.

Mites are a problem in beekeeping. Tracheal mites, for example, are microscopic, and they effect the bees by getting into their tracheal, or breathing tube. This can have disastrous outcomes, if it goes unnoticed for long enough.

Varroa mites are another kind of mite, that is more common than trachcal mites, and thought to be much more serious. These mites bite the bees, making their blood unhealthy, and giving them viruses. Varroa mites are very large, and they are to a bee as a basketball is to a person. Can you imagine having a bug, such as a tick, the size of a basketball on   your   back?

The most vile disease that affects bee's, is called American Foul Brood. This disease kills the brood before they get the chance to hatch, and the bees cannot live once they contract it. There is no known cure for American Foul Brood, so instead of treatment, there is a no tolerance policy. If your hive catches American Foul Brood, the only option is to burn all the frames and boxes involved in the hive, and pray that your other hives didn't catch it too.

An epidemic that is more terrifying than American Foul Brood, is Colony Collapse Disorder; or CCD. CCD has been spreading from coast to coast, and is causing trouble for beekeepers all over the world. CCD brings much attention to bee's in the mainstream media, however we have yet to find any solutions. The reason CCD is worse than American Foul Brood, is that unlike American Foul Brood, the reason for CCD is unknown. When CCD strikes, the majority of worker bees leave the hive, leaving behind only a few bees. It is a sad day for a beekeeper to find his hive empty. CCD is not only a problem for beekeepers, it is a problem for all of humanity.

What can really make a difference in the bee population? One thing that I believe can save the bees, is organic beekeeping. Mr. Eric had us do organic beekeeping, which is beekeeping in which very little chemicals are used, if at all. This form of beekeeping is better, safer, and healthier for the bees, as some chemicals cause the bees harm even if you may think they don't.

In organic beekeeping, not only do you use safe methods to assure that the bees do not have any problems, but you also use no chemicals in your yard or garden. Many chemicals that are meant for plants can be potentially deadly for bees. Certain poisonous dusts, meant for plants to keep pesky bugs from eating them, are very dangerous for bees. For example, one dust contains seven chemicals, six of the chemicals in it can harm bees, while the seventh attracts them. If you have a garden, be sure to double check and be absolutely positive that the chemical is not harmful to any pollinating insects, and if you cannot find any information on the label, there is a wide arrange available online. For those of you who love honey, organic beekeeping makes better honey as well! Who wants to eat honey full of chemicals?

5
WHY THEY MATTER

Why are disappearing bee's a problem for humanity? Can one little insect really make a difference in the lives of so many humans? In recent years, due to unfortunate reasons, much of the population has noticed bees in the news, in the paper, or in a movie such as "The Bee Movie". Even though bees are gaining more attention; if you talk to the average person, they will probably not really know much about the topic of what is happening to the bee population. Most people just worry about a bee flying around their head and want to kill it, others don't like them because of allergies, and others just think they are only good for making honey.

Bees are creatures that do so much for humanity,

and I hope one day they can be noticed for all they offer humanity. Bees make honey, wax, flowers, and food; yes, they make our food. Bees make as much as one third of your food, which makes quite the difference, if you ask me.

Bees pollinate much of the delicious foods people eat every day, and many of the beautiful flowers that we see. For example, bees pollinate almonds, cashews, strawberry's, broccoli, cabbage, peppers, oranges, cucumbers, and my favorite, blackberries. They even pollinate cotton!

The recent decline in honey bees has effected many people, not only beekeepers. Over two million dollars have been lost to dying or disappearing bees over the last 6 years. If we don't do something fast, our happy little bees may no longer be around for generations to come.

6
HOW TO BECOME A BEEKEEPER

Honey bees are disappearing in the wild, but you can still see them, and you probably have. They live in back yards, on roof tops, and in peoples gardens! In fact, your neighbor could have hives, and you don't even know it!

It is not as hard as you may think to become a beekeeper. Once you join the beekeeping community, you learn that there are many more beekeepers than you thought around you.

If you have a beekeeping association around you, then I would suggest joining it. The people in it will be very helpful, beekeepers are a true family. If you need help, they will make sure your colonies are okay, and guide you for more direction if needed.

There are many places you can buy the equipment needed for beekeeping. Many online catalogs and stores around you should offer the necessity's and the things you want and need for beekeeping.

Please be careful around bees, and make sure you respect them. They are truly harmless animals that are peaceful unless they are in an uncomfortable situation. You may get stung, but most of the time it's a last resort for a bee to sting. When a bee stings you it loses its life, therefor it has to be really scared to sting.

If you decide to become a beekeeper, make sure you research lots on the topic, it isn't always as easy as it seems, but it's not very hard either. The bee population doesn't lie in the hands of some big company that moves their bees around to pollinate crops all year, but in the hands of the backyard beekeepers who give their bees all the proper care and attention needed.

Happy Beekeeping

7
FUN FACTS

○ The Latin name for honey bees is apis Mellifera.

○ Honey bees are the state insect for 17 states, including the state I live in, North Carolina.

○ For effective pollination, there needs to be 60,000 bees working.

○ If a honey bee pollinates a plant, it will go to the same kind of plant until it returns to the hive.

○ The propolis that bees make for their hives can be made into glue.

○ It is thought that the ancient Egyptians, Romans, and Greeks, all kept bees.

○ Anybody, anywhere in the world can

keep bees.
- Bees see in ultraviolet colors.
- Bees extract honey and water through a tube used for extracting, called a proboscis.
- Bees have two sets of wings.
- Each wing has veins in it.
- Bees die if they go out in the rain.
- Bees sting you when they die.
- Bees have four stages of life, eggs, larvae, pupae, and adult.
- Bees fly when they reach 42 days old.
- Eggs are the size of the tip of a pen.
- It takes a queen 16 days to fully develop.
- The queen is the mother of all the bees in the hive.
- The queen is the only fully developed female, the worker bees are also female, and can develop if the queen is not laying properly, this is called a laying worker.
- An average of 100 bees die per hive every day.
- Foraging bees don't just bring back pollen, and nectar, they also bring back water, honey, and propolis.
- Bees cannot see red.
- There are 7,000 cells on one foundation.
- One bee visits 5,000 flowers every day.

- There are approximately 3.4 million bee hives in America.
- 1.5 million hives go to pollinating almond crops.
- Bees rob from other bees, this is common especially in the fall.

8
PICTURES

My nuke box, meant for raising queens.

Mr. Eric and I working bees.

Me observing a frame of bees.

Mr. Eric and I identifying eggs on a frame.

My hive as the bees are being kept.

Mr. Eric, another apprentice and I work bees.

Mr. Eric, another apprentice and I work bees.

ABOUT THE AUTHOR

Erica Miller was born on September 6th, 2001, in Carteret County, North Carolina. When she was 13, she learned about an apprentice ship program for Onslow county teenagers who were interested in beekeeping. She joined this program and soon became a full time beekeeper. She has 3 cats, a bird, 2 dogs, a fish, and hundreds of thousands of bees!